AF486427

VESTIGE

VESTIGE

poems

OLIVIA PIERCE GRAHAM

Press Pause Press

Vestige

Olivia Pierce Graham

Winner of the 2025 Beautiful Pause Prize

Published by:
Press Pause Press
Flying Fox Farm
279 Waters Road
Jacksonville, North Carolina 28546
www.presspausepress.org

Cover Design and Layout: Sofie Justice
Edited by: Victoria Lilley

ISBN: 979-8-9922406-8-9

Printed in the United States of America
First Press Pause Press Printing: March 2026

Pink leaking into gold, gold reflected on dark water,
a lesser version, a replica.

— Madeleine Cravens

Contents

Rapeseed
(an introduction)

It started as a diatribe.

A letter to the self, dictated

by some other self. Before the

safflower disappeared,

it was the rapeseed.

One by one by one.

Now, the dried ink speaks from

another realm. It seems that I've always

harbored these grave concerns and

frightening levels of elation.

My own raucous voice says

this should come as no surprise.

I'm still speculating about its hint of insincerity,

as if I could know sincerity by its sound.

Dysmenorrhea

That first menses smell. Wrists thin and
deep in a plot of wet black dirt, rife
with earthworms and isopods

fat enough to cut in half. Those little bodies;
little fibroids ruled benign. Transparent,
they recoil from the sun.

I contemplate killing just to see if I can.

The desire stirs atonal inside me,
swelling like a ruined violin.

Of course I can't.

Another day is half-complete,
another half-completion
is closer to the end.

The Riddle
(cento)

If you say I am a mystic,
then fine: I'm a mystic.
It leads to nothing else than what it started as.

I'm no messenger,
don't know the riddle, how
even the rain sweats, unkempt like the rest of us.

Her umbrella is just the extension
I know
to indicate
that certain information is still missing.

So it goes: the seer mistaken for the seen.
I hang my expectations out on a string
one by one, in a kind of line.

Detroit Beach

(erasure)

Stinging nostrils   the wind
A beach with lies and unexpected hours

The taste of   metal
spitting teeth   and sawdust
and always   the lies:

Blue exhalations glittering infinitesimally
A promise barefoot in the snow

The ashcan and flames
A red sea in which black coals embed   everything
wasteful   wrong

Flakes fall slow   steady
The waves growl

Ashore, your feet   in boots
Naked needles tarnish the thought
eclipsing you

Thunder coats the spoon—
the answer unloved
Not so   likeable

You found you could live   altogether blank
Blue
Definite

Anniversary

By then the house had collapsed.

February had thawed twice since.

I could have collapsed.

I could have fled when the squatters came.

They left their discard to rot the carpet.

Their chemical marks to stain the walls.

Two years is long enough.

It's plenty.

Nobody from now would have recognized me then.

That was me on the porch.

Dressed like a bad omen.

A former tenant broke in through the window.

I scattered roses on the lawn while his dogs growled.

Compartmentalization of Steam

A wealthy man pays my way enough for me to feel beholden
and now I'm in a swimsuit. We alternate between sauna and
steam room, Hell and Hotter Hell, and he finds the suffering
in each a luxury, his senses delightfully obscured.

Hearing assaulted with hiss; vision blinded by white
wisps of smoke. This is what it feels like
to turn into a ghost. I sit or think I'm sitting.
Condensation slips and sweats until everything
is wet and the same.

Skin never ends and surface
doesn't know where to begin.
I no longer have a body. His hand
goes to my thigh, but I've already disappeared.
His voice, long since drowned, sounds like the drone of insects.
I grow desperate wings and brittle little limbs.

Penmanship

I first beheld it at her dining room table
where the documents were lit by dusk,
the pile of them still as a cat,
almost sleeping.

Katya was there, shirking my superstitions.
I didn't know what I didn't know.

When the future came, I told her that I'd seen it
somewhere else before: iced atop an opulent cake
or weaved into its own constellation.

Vestige (Trileptal Poem)

nights my spirit
separates from me
sits up turbid &
surveys the room
my own body resting
heavy as a corpse beside
me on the pillow still
the empty orange bottles
encircle my head & create
a luminous crown

Wrists

An unfamiliar bed where consciousness departed like a zephyr
I awoke to find the discarded skin of a snake around my wrists

Deception became worth its weight in leather
My fists shook at my sides until I felt an ache throughout my wrists

I should have sensed it in the weather
Held up both my arms and found the strength to shout *my wrists*

Though the sex was only performative pleasure
An act to be endured while some new masculine weight held down my wrists

Blind to pre-oxygenated blue, partial to all that represents her
I couldn't get him to follow the map of veins that route my wrists

Aware that infatuation was a fruitless endeavor
I ripped the hair from my own scalp and tied a braid around my wrists

I tracked him down to show from where I let the venom
Made sure to tell him how I've always felt a certain way about my wrists

I dreaded the karmic receipt of my own vexatious treasure
Denied because it would mean an early grave to doubt my wrists

So abruptly did corporeal framework become foreign beyond measure
I looked down and noticed there was something strange about my wrists

Saturday

Saturday hardly gets to begin, and already there is
a motorist lying face down dead on Fort Street.
This has nothing to do with me, or you, but his body
looked as lifeless as yours once did while sleeping.
I've learned all about grey matter, how it starts to overflow
from the ears, dripping like some mug somewhere that I never got
to cradle close while walking towards you, offering a cup of hot black tea,
steam billowing from the hot black wreckage of my life. There is so much
sorrow to swallow. My father's brother killed by a man
who'd been imbibing too much whiskey. My father
said his mother's ghost looked just like spilled milk.
She made her first appearance gradually, then suddenly.
I became her namesake. She played the part of the moment
just before impact. I played the subsequent sirens.

Thespianism

You know the adage about those who mean everything they say:

they think everyone else does too.

I assumed you knew.

I assumed you were committed to our shared delusion.

You knew, too well, of youth and desperation.

How they're signed and sealed in digital envelopes.

I knew but denied all evidence of your turpitude;

Enamored, as it were.

You were gone before I could tell you what the critic told me:

That if I was going to fail, I should at least go down in flames.

Read too many books and your life will disappoint you. Your couch will be flannel,
the faucet will leak. The paintings on the wall all become fakes—Pollock's
splatter only flecks of mold. You wanted to love like a Nabokov,
scrawling furious prose and fainting at the sight. Putting too much perfume on
your envelopes.   How can you be spotlit by a television set? That's some other life.
You keep trying until you can't. Smudged black eyes and hasty red lips,
each curl falling like a poisoned sparrow.   In some novel,
you're always fretting about, on your way to some soiree. There's no parking
and the chauffeur loses his temper. You lose your kerchief while your date bites
your tongue in the rain. You get home late, cover yourselves in velvet,
the weight of your many sheets. You're thirsty and he reaches for the nightstand.
He remembers which glass is yours by the stain on the rim. Your mouth
is a wound so fresh you forget it's supposed to bleed.

Dirt

hypochondria sounds like   the name   of a   flower blossoms like
                every   un-   explained bruise   trembles
      with the   dew   of a cold   sweat   needs a constant
tending to lest you start   to wither   but if hypochondria is a   flower
            then hydrangea becomes   disease   because it is
      delicate   and deciduous   and toxic   shedding its petals
                                    planting seeds   and if
      hypochondria is a   flower   then   hypochondriac means
              that we'd need   no word   for gardener
                                                      you'd pick
                                              the stem   yourself
                                              watch the   ground
                                                  scab over

Untethered

I stare at the wall until my face is as blank
as its own. I've been thinking a lot about levitating.

How weightless I am when my tether to you
is frayed and then gone. I fail when searching

for simile. I metaphor instead:
Sidewalk litter tumbling schizophrenic.

A flock of birds that become collectively
smaller in the debris of afternoon.

Floating with no destination.
I fail when searching. I fray and then I'm gone.

Bygones

One-night stands find me mid-delirium
in the mirror, speaking unusual sentences.

*

Saved recordings breathe my name
from a liminal space. I keep one hand on my reflection,
sobbing something indecipherable in the dark.

*

Back home: crickets migrate towards the meadow,
feigning themselves fearless. They know how
to leave their dead there, dead.

*

I used to think it was your idea
to need me.

Wildfire, Still Burning

The slender necks of the does are bent
Eating ash and artichoke
From the garden. I sent you
Out into the smoke to see
For yourself. I wanted you to breathe
Canada burning and know
That there was nothing
You could do
Every broken promise, now a specimen
Jeweled in the amber
Of your mind

Back towards the sky, the bugs are
Calling out to you
Small beacons of light to guide you
Into the overgrown brush
All that olive green. Listen to
The birch trees that tell you
No, not one small thing
To address
Your betrayal, unflinching as a stone
Glistening like larvae in the stomach

Desired, We Would Suffer

(cento)

You don't survive a love letter from me.
Your mouth merely gargles its ghost. Airquotes understate,
vulnerable in a way that doesn't threaten.
Wasn't that you I saw slumming around there
with the dirt and rock from the neighborhood
knocking its clouds into the ashtray of the city?
She bowed and posed like she knew I needed a myth –
her tongue off its hinge, flopping.
I wondered if she'd laugh.
She could take for granted
a slow, slow tango in the empty bar and the dark
until she sleeps, when nothing else matters, when
her hair will be the sheen of brown you remember,
or had known all along or never.
I felt how it burned your flesh, burned for the two worlds to meet –
reticence which as you once said is merely
beautiful first, and ugly afterward.
Say what we will, at times it seems the rarest
moment of our being.
You write about the life that's vividest,
one from which no words escaped.
If I've learned anything, it's that I could be anywhere.
You follow the instructions, then
can stand so quietly in a room that the room appears empty.
The chair I'm sitting on is mostly nothing.
Whose idea was it?
Now that all the sweetness is gone, though we were the sweetness,
I am peering out from my own grave.
Dream is at once a heavy and delicate thing.
I hated the world's complicitous give,
sad and clear in what seemed always a perfect
unfastening. I hardly knew
the road that leads there, always beginning.
If there is only one world, it is this one.
No, let me make this real –
I don't know how to hold this truth,
to go back again and again, and throw
in my head and in my hollow.
To simply lie down and die. I am not that strong.
Out here, there's a bowing even the trees are doing
at the end of your book. I'm reading between the lines
as we speak, halfheartedly exploding.

Outpatient

My relishing of the minute hand begins at two. I gaze up
at the clock, a holy shrine. See how the beginning closes
in on the ending. A ballerina's perfect pirouette. A nickel,
a penny, a dime. I don't ask for much, just one rotation to
complete itself once. Someone to count to sixty sixty times.

Vestige (Trileptal Poem)

in offices they perpetuate pseudo-contemplation
extrapolation of *how much longer can this last* but it's already been
longer than I can endure I keep waking shocked & drenched my body's emission
a sickly-citrus scent that draws the flies to me I fish a hair from my mouth & succumb
comatose again it's come time to consult the tarot cards the palmistry charts   it's
come time to consult the dead knowledgeable in the ground they are twitching
tiny futon in the storage closet tainted millstream of the mind
I'm sleeping off the decadence in me

Non-Smoker

Hubris and novice always break the filter.
Too-forceful mouth and artless fingers.
Clumsy, fucked up things.

An old admirer once told me this:
Inhale the smoke quickly enough and the cancer
doesn't have time to get inside you.

I should have slept with him.
His first and last name together
translated roughly to *peaceful field*.

One where the pumpkins are covered
in frost and it is decidedly much
too late.

Abandonment in Four Haikus

pheromones ablaze

you once asked for a poem

never delivered

-

my legs asunder

immortalized in color

spine twisting in shame

-

my teeth grazed your throat

on West 58th and 9th

then I drove through rain

-

methodical grief

the fugue I'd live in for years

upon losing you

Fair Verona

this place looks like a house
built to eradicate your memories
into cobwebs wrecked with the breath
that I once felt
when I shivered as if covered
under the tatters of a blanket
where we were uncertain and
potent and new and
I was horrified
human underneath you
in an unfamiliar house

you'd live in with someone else
until they disintegrated
from your gentle mouth
tearing at me
with a thousand spiders fighting
beside your bedroom wall
where I stained your pillow bloody and
you refused to close your eyes
thinking about my body
weighted down
and waking up alone

Love Poem with Archery

Your hand recoils as if you've been burned
You take aim

I'm watching you practice to kill
Looking for the right word

You take aim
The arrow misses its target, like me

Looking for the right word
When I write a poem for you inside my head

The arrow misses its target, like me
Failing to describe this feeling adequately

When I write a poem for you inside my head
What I'm trying to say is that I'm

Failing to describe this feeling adequately
While I'm watching you

What I'm trying to say is that I'm
Wishing you were watching me

While I'm watching you
Sonnets and prose scatter like arrows

Wishing you were watching me
I'm all bleeding heart without a word inside my head

Sonnets and prose scatter like arrows
If I could condense it to a sentence

I'm all bleeding heart without a word inside my head
You're practicing to kill and still nothing is dead

If I could condense it to a sentence
I've lost my capacity for eloquence

You're practicing to kill and still nothing is dead
You pick up the arrow and try again

Husband

Morning sickness with a daily dose of juxtaposition
I'm gliding through the trail, hugging a heap of cotton
And spotting sandhill cranes

Dripping sweat and morbid fascination, I watch the mosquitoes
Penetrate our fetid flesh and feed. Spokes from buried farm equipment
Penetrate the earth. The earth reveals its terracotta
Rust rising reverent from the ground

A red cardinal, then its stunning predecessor, protect
A tree that's really more rot than bark. It houses their
Inconspicuous eggs in sharp twigs and broken leaves

Remember that I am telling you this days after I slept
Standing up, sloped against you

Exhibition

Two fingers take to a lymph node.
They're searching for a pulse.
I am back to inhabiting my body,
To calculating the rate of this textured existence.

A statue before me has her marble arms
Outstretched. I relate to this well, her
Immaculate and enviable affliction.

A recipe for missing my maladaptation.
An old friend interrupts this thought;
he tells me my first book is on his shelf,
collecting dividends.

This is incorrect; a malapropism, of course,
But an example of the wrong thing
Sounding right. In the garden,

Others emit their own improper utterances.
Their shallow voices stay protected, sheltered
under vascular plants in dim light.

Gleeful Rejection of Object Permanence

Of the boarding process and its reliably plastic smell.
Give me stilted interactions with the nameless hundreds,
in droves, arriving—their luggage looming
enigmatic and impersonal.

Stock photo public people, never seen asleep in front
of the television. Never carefully peeling an orange.
I'm in my window seat, trying to picture it.

Above the gossamer, they are with me.
Sitting up straight, facing forward; when I leave here,
they'll be nothing. Floating fabric on invisible bones,
disembodied voices upstaged by the turbine.

Coveted anonymity. An absence to be replenished.
How perfect they are. How I'd never want to know them.

Secondary Locations

Wherever bodies are comprised of bones
and blanks, their shelters are seldom more than the
indents where they sleep. They rest below the
folds of curtains. They capture all
confabulations. They block out the sun. It's true
that I'm a walking case of déjà vu, oft mistaken
for being jaded. Believe me when I say I've
endured this all before: Brick buildings and
multi-story structures. Birdbaths outside
without a single ripple. Smokestacks standing
resolute because they know they're welcome
company.

Vestige (Lamictal Poem)

I envied the tree or I suppose
anything that was rooted to the ground
the texture of solid bark evidence of the atoms
& molecules comprising it too tangible for touch
or maybe too well-formed to comprehend as I unfolded
to the field vapor unto fleeting vapor the face of each distant
house held in solemn observance stoic remembrance they knew
just why they could see right through me churning into
smog holding onto the branch so I wouldn't dis-
appear the result of titration & patience &
patience the schedule is strict each day
is broken into perforated pieces

The Riddle [Reprise]
(cento)

And what now—
stirred, swaying
umbrella that's always with her,

when was it I gathered that dissolve
resists you and then ceases to resist?

Now the stifling days disrobe.
Now I hear the good voices.
They fall fast in freezing mist.

Oh, yes, the rain is sorry. Unfemale, of course, the rain is

If Your Name Was Ruby

I leave the orchestra behind. Later I'll wake to your absence. The grandfather clock will remind me that I've only lived another hour, that I'm not yet dead, albeit stripping the minutes sensually. Flaunting ratty undergarments,   somewhere you're out there writhing. Fabric that never contains all that muscle and strength, your jawline sharp as a fang, abdomen undulating like a starving serpent. Freckled girl, I want to touch your legs. Your lips and their faded fuchsia underneath your lipstick, their whatever-you-call-that shade of red.   I am learning to live with the idea. I am cramping and coping. I won't rip your hair from any drain, nor dodge diluted drops of your blood on a bathroom floor.   There is no house with an oak tree, no canary chirping for its life from a wrought-iron cage. Sucked in your mind-mud, you'll never know nor forget me. Your fleeting face unearths only now and then in a dream.   I console myself and call you vapid, ungrateful for these gifted images that disintegrate now as I wake: Tiny malnourished beaks. Matted feathers shining yellow. Dozens of beady eyes black as garnet, or—I bet you didn't know— even gold.

Acknowledgements

So much love and gratitude to the editors of the publications
in which the following poems first appeared, sometimes in earlier versions:

Beyond Words Magazine: "Non-Smoker"
Button Eye Review: "If Your Name Was Vera"
Cathexis Northwest Press: "Saturday"
Killer Nashville Magazine: "Rapeseed"
Midsummer Dream House: "Compartmentalization of Steam"
Ohm Journal: "Detroit Beach"
Oroboro: "Dirt" and "Vestige (Buspirone Poem)"
River & South Review: "Dysmenorrhea"
Sad Girl Diaries: "Gleeful Rejection of Object Permanence"
Wild Roof Journal: "If Your Name Was Ruby"

Further love and gratitude to the editors of the publications
who gave the following poems special recognition:

"Gleeful Rejection of Object Permanence" was selected as the third runner-up in
Sad Girl Diaries' 2021 Summer Poetry Contest.

Though not published with them, "Compartmentalization of Steam" made the shortlist for
Fatal Flaw Literary Magazine's 2024 Poetry Contest.

The poem "The Riddle" is a cento poem.
The poem's individual lines are sourced from the following poems in consecutive order:

"Midnight Office" – **Cynthia Cruz**
"Midnight Office" – **Cynthia Cruz**
"Friend"– **Jana Prikryl**
"Sibyl" – **Jana Prikryl**
"Magical" – **Cynthia Cruz**
"Phnom Penh Diptych: Wet Season" – **Jenny Xie**
"Umbrella Photo Poems" – **Elaine Equi**
"Yu y tu" – **Elaine Equi**
"Yu y tu" – **Elaine Equi**
"Cut to the Chase" – **Elaine Equi**
"Inwardly" – **Jenny Xie**
"Phnom Penh Diptych: Dry Season" – **Jenny Xie**
"Phnom Penh Diptych: Dry Season" – **Jenny Xie**

The poem "Detroit Beach" is an erasure poem which uses
"The Crystal Lithium" by **James Schuyler** as its source material.

The poem "Desired, We Would Suffer" is a cento poem.

The poem's title is sourced from the poem "Wild Thing" by **Nickole Brown**.

The poem's individual lines are sourced from the following poems in consecutive order:

"Ricky Martin on Homosexuality" – **Julian Talamantez Brolaski**
"Alfred North Whitehead" – **Gregory Pardlo**
"Man in a Window" – **Ralph Angel**
"Tomorrow" – **William Olsen**
"In Heaven" – **Matthew Dickman**
"Elegy to a Goldfish" – **Matthew Dickman**
"Wonder Woman" – **Ada Limón**
"Wild Thing" – **Nickole Brown**
"My Father's Loveletters" – **Yusef Komunyakaa**
"Old-fashioned" – **Dara Wier**
"Shore Leave – **Lynda Hull**
"Adolescence" – **Larry Levis**
"We Never Close" – **David Clewell**
"Old-fashioned" – **Dara Wier**
"Silver Lake" – **Brigit Pegeen Kelly**
"On Waking After Dreaming of Raoul" – **Lynn Emanuel**
"The Condom Tree" – **Chase Twichell**
"Inspiration" – **Sherod Santos**
"The Cleaving" – **Li-Young Lee**
"Ground Swell" – **Mark Jarman**
"Old-fashioned" – **Dara Wier**
"In Defense of Small Towns" – **Oliver de la Paz**
"Eating Walnuts" – **Jennifer Keith**
"Antebellum House Party" – **Terrance Hayes**
"The Macarena" – **Ed Skoog**
"The Gypsy" – **Susan Stewart**
"In Heaven" – **Matthew Dickman**
"The Madness of King George" – **Matthew Dickman**
"Museum" – **Sydney Lea**
"Cherry Bombs" – **Alice Fulton**
"The Widening Spell of the Leaves" – **Larry Levis**
"Salmon" – **Jorie Graham**
"The River Has No Hair To Hold Onto" – **Ralph Angel**
"Decrescendo" – **Larry Levis**
"Against Despair: The Kid Goat" – **Nickole Brown**
"Killing Methods" – **Ada Limón**
"The Plunge" – **Ada Limón**
"The Noisiness of Sleep" – **Ada Limón**
"Home Fires" – **Ada Limón**
"Dead Stars" – **Ada Limón**
"This Book Belongs to Susan Someone" – **David Clewell**
"When at a Certain Party in NYC" – **Erin Belieu**

The poem "The Riddle (Reprise)" is a cento poem.
The poems' individual lines are sourced from the following poems in consecutive order:

"Tending" – **Jenny Xie**
"Bender" – **Jana Prikryl**
"Umbrella Photo Poems" – **Elaine Equi**
"Murder" – **Jana Prikryl**
"Anonymous" – **Jana Prikryl**
"Epistle" – **Jenny Xie**
"Après Coup" – **Cynthia Cruz**
"The Hustler's Love: A Perfection of Sacred Lust to Stillness Quietry" – **Lawrence W. Manglitz**
"Project for a Fainting" – **Brenda Shaughnessy**

The line "under vascular plants and dim light"
in the poem
"Exhibition"
is inspired by the title of the paper
"Rationale: Photosynthesis of Vascular Plants in Dim Light,"
which was authored by **Xialoin Wang et al.**,
and published in the peer-reviewed journal
Frontiers in Plant Science in 2020.

"Fair Verona" is the iconic setting for **Shakespeare's *Romeo and Juliet***, introduced in the Prologue as the location for a "long-standing feud" between the Montague and Capulet families. This Italian city serves as the backdrop for the tragedy of the "star-cross'd lovers".

Adorations

The New School's MFA Creative Writing faculty

The New School's MFA Creative Writing Class of 2022 cohort

Kolleen Carney Hoepfner

Nathaniel Santiago

SE Harsha

Co-workers

Parents of all varieties

^ Ditto siblings

Dogs

Brooke

Husband

About the Author

Olivia Pierce Graham holds an MFA in Poetry from The New School, where she was a recipient of the Paul Violi Poetry Prize. She is the author of *Gloom of Excruciating Desires* (winner of *Cherry Dress Chapbooks'* Debut Chapbook Prize, 2022), and currently serves as Acquisitions Editor for *Lit Fox Books* and Author Interviews Editor for *Austin Poetry Review*. She is married to the best person in the world.

www.ingramcontent.com/pod-product-compliance
Lightning Source LLC
Chambersburg PA
CBHW061316140726
47998CB00006B/2414